LETTERS FROM AROUND THE WORLD

CHINA

Julia Waterlow

Photographs by Howard Davies

CHERRYTREE BOOKS

Titles in this series

AUSTRALIA · BANGLADESH · BRAZIL · CANADA · CHINA
COSTA RICA · EGYPT · FRANCE · GERMANY · GREECE · INDIA
INDONESIA · IRELAND · ITALY · JAMAICA · JAPAN · KENYA
MEXICO · NIGERIA · PAKISTAN · POLAND · RUSSIA
SAUDI ARABIA · SOUTH AFRICA · SPAIN · SWEDEN · THE USA

A Cherrytree Book

Conceived and produced by

Nutshell
MEDIA

www.nutshellmedialtd.co.uk

First published in paperback in 2009 by
Evans Brothers Ltd
2A Portman Mansions
Chiltern Street
London W1U 6NR

Editor: Polly Goodman
Design: Mayer Media Ltd
Map artwork: Encompass Graphics Ltd
All other artwork: Mayer Media Ltd

All photographs were set up and taken by Howard Davies,
except: p29 (Great Wall and giant panda) Wayland Picture
Library (Gordon Clements).

Acknowledgements
The photographer would like to thank the following for all
their help with this book: Yi-yi, her parents Jing Ru and Dr
Lian, and her grandparents Yi Xian Gao and Su Sheng Min;
Wu Xue Song for excellent interpreting; and Michelle
Ballance and Sean White for their help in the UK.

British Library Cataloguing in Publication Data
Waterlow, Julia
    China. – (Letters from around the world)
    1. China - Social conditions - 1976 - Juvenile literature
    2. China - Social life and customs - 1976 -
Juvenile literature
    I. Title
    951'.06

ISBN-13: 978-1842345337

Cover: Yi-yi and her friends on the Qingdao seafront.
Title page: Yi-yi and a classmate practise the *pi-pa*.
This page: Zhanqiao Pier stretches out into Qingdao Bay.
Contents page: Toffee apples for sale on the beach.
Glossary page: Yi-yi practises writing Chinese characters.
Further information page: T'ai chi in the park.
Index: Skipping games in the school playground.

Contents

My Country

Tuesday, 8 January

7 Pijiu Road
Qingdao 220066
Shandong
China

Dear Kim,

Ni hao! (You say 'nee-how' – that's 'hello' in Chinese.)

My name is Lian Yin. In China we put our surname first, so you can call me Yin, or Yi-yi, which is my nickname. Yi-yi means 'ripple'. I'm 8 years old. I live in the city of Qingdao, in China. Qingdao is in the north of China, by the sea.

I'll write again soon and tell you more about me and my family.

From
Yi-yi

This is me with my mum and dad, walking down the street in Qingdao.

4

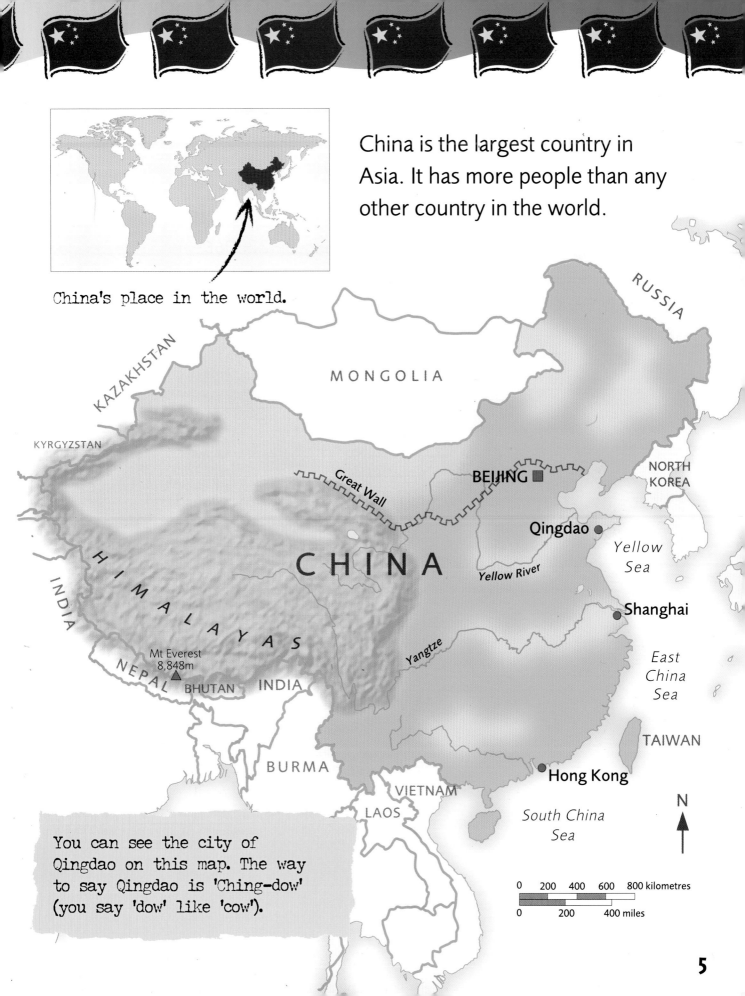

China is the largest country in Asia. It has more people than any other country in the world.

China's place in the world.

RUSSIA

KAZAKHSTAN

KYRGYZSTAN

MONGOLIA

Great Wall

BEIJING

Qingdao

NORTH KOREA

Yellow Sea

CHINA

Yellow River

Shanghai

HIMALAYAS

INDIA

Mt Everest 8,848m

NEPAL

BHUTAN

INDIA

Yangtze

East China Sea

TAIWAN

BURMA

Hong Kong

VIETNAM

LAOS

South China Sea

N

You can see the city of Qingdao on this map. The way to say Qingdao is 'Ching-dow' (you say 'dow' like 'cow').

| 0 | 200 | 400 | 600 | 800 kilometres |

| 0 | 200 | 400 miles |

Qingdao is a very busy and crowded city. About 2.9 million people live there. The city is an important port. Big ships come and go from the Yellow Sea. There are many high-rise buildings and large factories.

The city is famous for making beer. It is also well-known for bottling mineral water, which is collected from Laoshan, a mountain nearby.

Qingdao is growing fast and there are lots of new high-rise buildings.

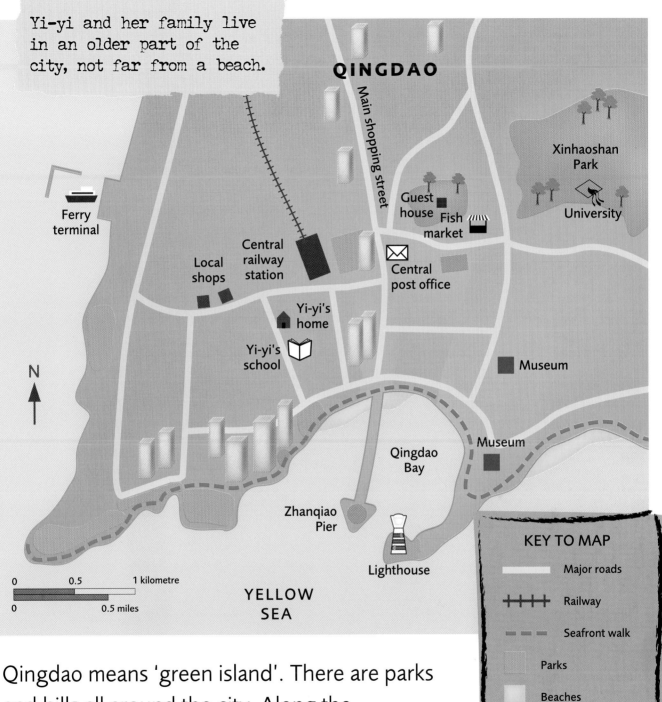

Yi-yi and her family live in an older part of the city, not far from a beach.

QINGDAO

Main shopping street

Ferry terminal

Central railway station

Local shops

Yi-yi's home

Yi-yi's school

Guest house

Fish market

Central post office

Xinhaoshan Park

University

Museum

N

Museum

Qingdao Bay

Zhanqiao Pier

Lighthouse

YELLOW SEA

0   0.5   1 kilometre

0   0.5 miles

KEY TO MAP

Major roads

Railway

Seafront walk

Parks

Beaches

High-rise buildings

Built-up area

Qingdao means 'green island'. There are parks and hills all around the city. Along the waterfront there are sandy beaches and seafront walks. People spend their free time there. Many people like to visit Zhanqiao Pier, which stretches out into Qingdao Bay.

Landscape and Weather

Qingdao is surrounded on three sides by the Yellow Sea. Not far from the city is Laoshan, a mountain with many paths, waterfalls and caves.

A woman collects food for her animals on Laoshan.

Qingdao is a popular tourist resort because of its sandy beaches and pleasant weather. People travel from all over China to have a holiday there.

Northern China can be very hot in the summer and freezing cold in winter. Qingdao is not as hot or as cold because the sea warms the city in winter and cools it in summer.

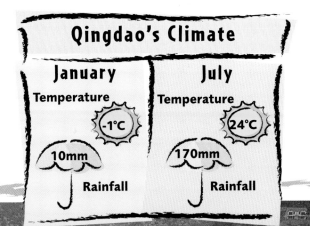

Qingdao's Climate

January	July
Temperature	Temperature
-1°C	24°C
10mm	170mm
Rainfall	Rainfall

The sea is very important to the people living near Qingdao. These fishing families are sorting out their catch of shellfish.

At Home

Yi-yi does not have any brothers and sisters. Many families in China have only one child to stop the population from growing too quickly. Yi-yi has grandparents who also live in Qingdao.

Yi-yi puts vegetables in the pan for supper. The pan is called a wok.

Yi-yi and her parents live in a flat. They have two bedrooms, a kitchen, a bathroom and a living room. There are so many people in Qingdao that most people have to live in flats.

Yi-yi often helps her mum clean the flat.

Yi-yi's mum teaches her how to play Chinese chess on the living-room table. The chess pieces are made of wood and have their Chinese names written on them.

Yi-yi has a computer in her bedroom.

Yi-yi has her own bedroom, where she does her homework and keeps her toys. The family has a television and video in the living room. There is a fridge and a washing machine in their small kitchen.

Yi-yi is in the kitchen learning how to stir noodles using chopsticks.

Thursday, 7 March

7 Pijiu Road
Qingdao 220066
Shandong
China

Dear Kim,

Thanks for your letter last week. Have I told you about my flat? It's five floors up so I have lots of stairs to climb! We have a big table in our living room where we eat our meals. I also use the table for playing games with my friends. It's great for making paper silhouettes – my favourite hobby. We cut out paper shapes or patterns and stick them on to card.

What's your home like? Write back soon and tell me about it.

From
Yi-yi

Here I am making paper silhouettes with my best friend Meng Yuan.

Food and Mealtimes

For breakfast, Yi-yi usually has a glass of milk and an egg. For lunch she has noodles or dumplings, followed by fruit. The family eats together in the evening.

Both Yi-yi's parents like cooking and she loves helping. They make several dishes, put them in the middle of the table and help themselves with their chopsticks.

For the evening meal there's always fish and rice, as well as vegetables.

At the supermarket, the fish are kept alive in a tank. Yi-yi is choosing the one she wants to buy.

Yi-yi's family buys fresh food from shops or markets near their house. Once a week they go to the large supermarket, which is a few kilometres away.

Crunchy crabs on sticks are a tasty snack.

Saturday, 4 May

7 Pijiu Road
Qingdao 220066
Shandong
China

Hi Kim!

You asked for a recipe for a Chinese dish. Here's how to make *jiaozi*. They're a sort of dumpling.

You will need: 250g flour, 1 egg, a pinch of salt, 4 tablespoons water, 300g minced pork, 4 spring onions (finely chopped), 1 tablespoon soya sauce, 2 crushed cloves of garlic, 1 teaspoon powdered ginger

1. Mix the flour, egg, salt and water together in a bowl. Knead the mixture well to make a smooth, thick dough.
2. Roll small pieces of dough into balls 2–3cm wide. Then roll out the balls into thin, round mini-pancakes.
3. In another bowl mix the pork, spring onions, soya sauce, garlic and ginger.

Here Granny is rolling out the dough into little pancakes.

Now we're putting in the filling.

4. Put a teaspoon of the mixture in the centre of each mini-pancake. Fold the pancake over to make a semicircle and pinch the edges together.

5. Fill a big pan with water and bring it to the boil.
6. Carefully put the *jiaozi* in the pan and boil for 10 minutes. Give them a gentle stir so they don't stick together.

We always use pork, but you could leave it out and make up your own filling. You could add chopped mushrooms, other vegetables and different spices. Try them and let me know what you think.

From

Yi-yi

Finished! The *jiaozi* are ready to cook.

School Day

On school days, Yi-yi gets up at 7 a.m. She goes to the primary school near her home. Classes start at 8 a.m. The main subjects are Chinese, English, handwriting, maths and music. There are exercises or sports every day.

Yi-yi walks to school with her friends every day. It only takes her 5 minutes to get there.

The children in Yi-yi's class wear red scarves to show they are Young Pioneers, young members of the Communist Party.

On Monday mornings the school has assembly and the children sing the Chinese national anthem. Yi-yi goes to her aunt and uncle's house nearby for lunch. Some children have lunch at school.

After lunch the children skip in the playground before lessons start again.

Yi-yi is learning to play the *pi-pa*, a traditional Chinese instrument.

When school finishes at 4 p.m., Yi-yi stays at her aunt and uncle's house until her parents finish work. When she gets home, Yi-yi does about half an hour of homework.

Yi-yi listens to a tape for her English homework.

Sunday, 17 July

7 Pijiu Road
Qingdao 220066
Shandong
China

Dear Kim,

I'm glad to hear you did well in your maths test. I really like maths. My English is getting better, isn't it? I have extra English lessons every Sunday. You're lucky only having school for five days a week.

Do you learn another language? Chinese is quite different from English. Our words are called characters. Each one is like a little picture and I have to learn them all by heart.

Write soon!

From

Yi-yi

Here I am practising writing Chinese characters.

Off to Work

Like most women in China, Yi-yi's mum goes to work. She makes television programmes at Qingdao Television Centre. Yi-yi's dad is a surgeon in a hospital.

Both Yi-yi's parents take a bus to work because they have to travel a long way across the city. Not many people in China have cars. Most people use buses, bicycles or taxis.

Yi-yi's mum interviews a local businessman in the television studios.

This man makes money by selling toffee-apples to tourists on the beach.

Many people in Qingdao work in factories, or in the fishing industry. Others work in the tourist industry. Outside the city, farmers grow wheat, maize and millet, as well as peanuts, tobacco and cotton.

Traditional fishing boats being built near Qingdao.

Free Time

If the weather is fine, Yi-yi takes her scooter to the seafront with her friends. At home, she likes to play games on her computer and watch cartoons on television.

Yi-yi rides her scooter on the seafront.

At weekends, Yi-yi and her parents go to one of Qingdao's beaches or parks, or visit Yi-yi's grandparents for a meal.

These women are practising t'ai chi, a kind of gentle martial art.

Few people in the city have gardens, so the beaches and parks are usually crowded. Wherever there is some open space, people like to play sports such as basketball, or practise martial arts such as t'ai chi.

Yi-yi's dad is teaching her calligraphy — painting Chinese characters with a brush. It is a great art in China.

Religion and Festivals

This is a statue of the Buddha, in a Buddhist temple.

The main religion in China is Buddhism. Like many Chinese people, Yi-yi's family are not religious, but they enjoy the traditional festivals.

The biggest festival in China is the Spring Festival, at the start of the Chinese New Year.

Yi-yi and her family visit her grandparents for a meal at Spring Festival.

Monday, 9 February

7 Pijiu Road
Qingdao 220066
Shandong
China

Ni hao Kim!

It's been really exciting here this week because it's the Spring Festival. This is my favourite time of year. We decorated our house and visited our family and friends. We ate lots of special food (like *jiaozi*) and sweets. There was lion and dragon dancing in the streets, where people join together in giant lion and dragon costumes. There were the loudest firecrackers you've ever heard! It was really noisy but good fun!

From

Yi-yi

This is Grandpa giving me a red envelope with 'lucky' money in it for the Spring Festival. I bow and thank him when I receive it.

Fact File

Population: About 1.3 billion, more than any other country. Chinese families are asked to have only one child to stop the population growing too quickly.

Capital city: The capital of China is Beijing, which is the second-largest city. Shanghai is China's largest city.

Size: 9,597,000km^2. China is the third-largest country in the world.

Flag: The Chinese flag is red with five stars. The big star represents the Communist Party. The others represent soldiers, farmers, workers and students.

Main religions: There is no official religion in China, but many people are Buddhists. A small number of people are Muslim or Christian.

Currency: Yuan (divided into fen). 100 fen =1 yuan.

Languages: Most people speak Mandarin Chinese, although there are other kinds of Chinese such as Cantonese.

Highest mountain: Mount Everest (Mount Qomolangma in Chinese). It is 8,848m high.

Longest river: The Yangtze (Chang Jiang in Chinese) is 6,300km long. It is the world's third-longest river. Ships travel from the sea far into China along the Yangtze.

Famous landmark: The Great Wall of China is about 6,000km long. It was built across northern China to keep out invaders. Some parts of the wall were built over 2,000 years ago.

Famous people: Confucius was a wise man who lived about 2,500 years ago. Mao Zedong (1893–1976) was the leader of China for many years. He helped set up the Communist Party in China.

Main festivals: The Spring Festival, which is also called Chinese New Year, is in January or February. Each New Year is given the name of an animal. Other festivals are Qing Ming, the Moon Festival, National Day and Children's Day.

Wildlife: Giant pandas are only found in China. They are very rare so they are protected.

Stamps: Chinese stamps often show something about Chinese life, a famous place or wildlife. These stamps show traditional Chinese art, music, landscapes and flowers.

Inventions: The Chinese invented paper, gunpowder, silk, the magnetic compass, fireworks, porcelain and printing.

Glossary

Buddhism A religion started by the Buddha, a holy man from northern India, over 2,500 years ago.

chopsticks A pair of thin sticks used by the Chinese to pick up food.

Communist Party The main political party in China. Communists believe everything should be shared out equally among all the people.

dumplings Small pieces of cooked dough, sometimes made with a filling such as meat or vegetables.

firecrackers Small fireworks that make a loud bang when they go off.

martial arts Self-defence exercises using special movements and breathing. The movements can be hard and fast, like kung fu, or soft and slow, like t'ai chi.

national anthem A country's own special song.

noodles Food made from flour, rather like long, thin pasta.

population The number of people that live in a country.

silhouettes Outline shapes of something.

spice Something used in cooking to add flavour to food.

Spring Festival Also called Chinese New Year. It is held in January or February every year.

surgeon A doctor who does operations on people.

temple A building where people go to pray.

tourist industry Types of work to do with tourists.

tourist resort A place where people go on holiday.

traditional A word that describes something that has been done in a certain way for a very long time.

Further Information

Information books:

The Changing Face of China by Stephen Keeler (Wayland, 2007)

Countries of the World: China by Carole Goddard (Evans Brothers, 2007)

Country Insights: China by Julia Waterlow (Wayland, 2006)

C is for China by Sungwan So (Frances Lincoln, 2006)

Destination Detectives: China by Ali Brownlie Bojang (Raintree, 2005)

Festivals and Food: China by Amy Shui and Stuart Thompson (Wayland, 2006)

Food Around the World: China by Polly Goodman (Wayland, 2006)

A Visit to China by Peter and Connie Roop (Heinemann, 2008)

World in Focus: China by Ali Brownlie Bojang (Wayland, 2006)

A World of Festivals: Chinese New Year by Catherine Chambers (Evans Brothers, 2004)

Fiction:

The Dragon Painter by Rosie Dickins (Usborne, 2006)

The Emperor and the Nightingale by Hans Christian Andersen (Usborne, 2007)

Traditional Strories from China by Saviour Pirotta (Wayland, 2006)

Websites:

CIA World Factbook
https://www.cia.gov/library/publications/the-world-factbook/
Facts and figures about China and other countries.

Mama Lisa's World
www.mamalisa.com
Children's songs from China and other countries around the world.

Index